The Sixth Sense II

An easy-to-use lesson plan for teaching mainstream students about autism, with perspective-taking exercises that focus on the five senses and the sixth "social" sense

By Carol Gray

Award-winning author and creator of Social Stories™

The Sixth Sense II

All marketing and publishing rights guaranteed to and reserved by

FUTURE HORIZONS INC.

721 W. Abram Street
Arlington, Texas 76013
800-489-0727
817-277-0727
817-277-2270 (fax)
www.FHautism.com
E-mail: info@FHautism.com

Illustrations by Microsoft Word ClipArt & Art Explosion, Nova Development.

Originally created for Jenison Public Schools, Jenison, Michigan, USA.

Printed in the United States of America.

ISBN 10: 1-885477-90-2
ISBN 13: 978-1-885477-90-3

To all children, with respect for their natural curiosity about others.

My sincere appreciation to
Karen Lind, Sue Jonker, and Laurel Hoekman
for their critical review and assistance with
The Sixth Sense II,
and to my husband, Brian Gray, for his unfaltering encouragement.

Table of Contents

Preface

During the last decade, the identification of children with autism spectrum disorders (ASD) has resulted in an increasing awareness of their unique social challenges. Children diagnosed with high functioning autism and Asperger Syndrome are often included in general education settings. Here, they struggle to cope with the many interactions and social situations that comprise each school day; sometimes demonstrating unique responses that capture the attention, curiosity, and/or wariness of their classmates. The behavior of a child with ASD can be puzzling: *Why does this new classmate - who uses big words and knows so much about dinosaurs - never answer when we say "Hi"?*

In his book, *The Friendship Factor* (2002), Kenneth Rubin Ph.D. summarizes over twenty years of research on social and emotional development in childhood and the critical role of parents in helping their child "navigate the social world". Dr. Rubin indicates that by age of six or seven, children begin to make social comparisons, noting their own strengths and weaknesses relative to their peers. As a child's world expands from "me" to "me and everyone else", the social map adds increasing detail. Children who have unique responses will be noticed and questions will arise. Without answers, children may begin to believe it's wrong to ask - or come to unguided social conclusions of their own. The question is not, "Should we tell John's classmates that he has unique challenges?" when they, most likely, already *know* John responds differently to many situations. Ultimately, the question is much broader. How can we create a learning environment where all children feel socially safe and comfortable?

In 1993, *The Sixth Sense* was developed to share information about autism spectrum disorders with general education students, to explain behaviors that might otherwise be misinterpreted as frightening, odd, or rude. Originally published as part of *Taming the Recess Jungle* (Gray, 1993), the rationale was that students would be better equipped to include a classmate with unique behaviors when provided with accurate social information. Using the five senses as a frame of reference, the original *Sixth Sense* introduced students to their sixth - or social - sense via activities and discussion.

The Sixth Sense II is more comprehensive than its predecessor and appropriate for elementary students ages 7-12. The lesson plan is comprised of six segments:
1) Introduction
2) Review of the 5 Senses
3) Perspective-taking and the Sixth Sense
4) What is it like to have a Sixth Sense impairment?
5) How can we help?
6) Summary

Unlike the original lesson plan, The Sixth Sense II includes two appendixes that further expand and update the information. *Appendix A: Frequently Asked Questions and Answers* provides parents and professionals with information they will need to implement The Sixth Sense II, including ideas to reinforce the concepts with related activities. *Appendix B: Related Resources* lists and describes materials to enhance efforts to create and maintain a positive social environment. In addition to sharing new information in the appendixes, we are also *recruiting* new ideas from you. The form titled *The Sixth Sense II ...and YOU* on page 22 is an invitation to provide us with your feedback and suggestions.

It is our hope that The Sixth Sense II will continue the work of the original: To promote understanding and supportive social climates for children with autism spectrum disorders.

The Sixth Sense II

- Carol Gray, Consultant to Students with Autistic Spectrum Disorders

Goal: To improve student understanding and support of classmates with autistic spectrum disorders.

Objectives:

1) Students will identify how the five senses help us gather information

2) Students will list ideas to assist a classmate with a visual or hearing impairment

3) Students will learn how people make guesses about what others perceive, know and feel

4) Students will describe why our "social sense" may be considered "the sixth sense"

5) Students will describe the challenges experienced by children with visual/hearing impairments

6) Students will identify possible challenges experienced by a classmate who has a social-communication impairment

8) Students will list ideas to assist a classmate with a social-communication impairment

Materials:

1) Small item to hide (teddy bear)

2) Chalk, laminate board or overhead projector

3) Large photos or drawings of: eye, nose, mouth, ear, hand; children playing sports; and/or photos depicting basic emotions

Time to Implement: One to two hours. Several lists are created - do not erase until lesson is completed.

Important Note: Discuss The Sixth Sense II with the parents of the child with the autistic spectrum disorder (ASD) in advance. It is likely that parents will have questions, or that modifications will be required to tailor the lesson. For more information, see Appendix A: Answers to Frequently Asked Questions, and Appendix B: Related Resources.

Directions appear in plain text. *Italics* are used to indicate suggested script.

Introduction

Today I am going to share some important information with you about your classmate, _____. I am sure you have noticed that like you, _____ (likes to) (is interested in) _____. Like you, _____ does many things well. And, like you, _____ sometimes needs help. _____ needs help working and playing with others. We can help. The first step is to understand why working and playing with others is sometimes more difficult for_____. Listen carefully to this information. I know it will give you some ideas as to how we can help _____. Your ideas will be important as we work together to develop a plan to assist_____.

Review of the Five Senses:

A review of the five senses: sight, hearing, taste, smell, and touch provide a backdrop of familiar information prior to the introduction of Sixth Sense concepts. Lead a discussion of the five basic senses. Use photos/drawings to enhance the discussion. At the same time list/answer the following:

    1) What information do you gather with your sense of _____?

    2) Did anyone teach you how to see/hear/taste/touch/smell?

Next, focus on vision and hearing. Add to the lists of vision and hearing with discussion of the following:

    3) What would it be like without the ability to see/hear?

    4) What could you do to help a classmate who could not see/hear?

What follows is a sample list for sight with an accompanying illustration:

Sight

1. Helps us to see where we are going, read, keep safe, play ball, find things
2. No one teaches us to see. Sight is a "sense".
3. People who cannot see:
   - might need help to get around safely.
   - cannot read as most people do
4. Ideas to help a classmate who can't see:
   - Braille
   - help them on the playground
   - keep things in their place in the classroom

Perspective-taking and the Sixth Sense

The discussion of the five senses – and the information they provide - creates a natural introduction to the Sixth Sense. The lesson proceeds with a demonstration of how we also know what *other* people can see, hear, touch, taste, or smell.   Two perspective-taking activities help students discover how we can assume another person's perceptual (sensory) and cognitive (what others know) perspective by making very accurate guesses. A third activity explores the clues to the feelings of others (affective perspective).

We've listed the five senses on the board. No one taught you to see, hear, touch, taste, or smell. You also have a social sense – some abilities that help you to work and play with others. I'll show you how the social sense works.

Perceptual perspective-taking activity:

In this activity, students discover their ability to "see the world" through another person's eyes; to accurately identify what someone can see, hear, taste, smell, and/or touch, even from a distance. Still focusing on the basic senses, in this activity children discover that their knowledge of what other people perceive provides them with valuable information. This activity is based on the work of Dawson & Fernald (1987).

- Ask for a student volunteer from the back half of the classroom. Direct this student to remain seated.
- Ask that student to briefly describe things he/she can see from his/her seat. For example, the student may identify the board, classroom clock, or posters.
- Ask the student to identify things YOU see. The student may identify the students, their desks, the bulletin board display at the back of the classroom, etc.
- Identify items that are behind you, for example, the chalkboard and clock.   Facing the student with your back to those items, ask the student if you can see them from your current position. The student should reply in the negative. Ask the student, *How did you do that? How did you know what I can see?*

We know what others can see, hear, smell, taste, or touch, even if we are not right there with them. Did someone teach you to do that, or did you "just know"?

Record this information in the center of the chalkboard as illustrated at the top of the next page:

3

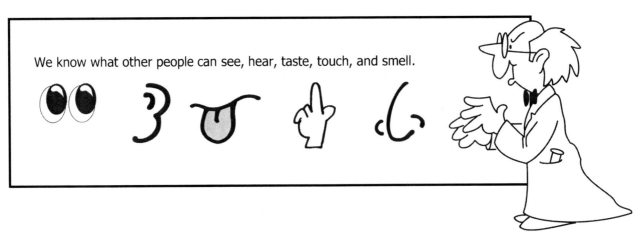

We know what other people can see, hear, taste, touch, and smell.

<u>Cognitive perspective-taking activity</u> (based on Baron-Cohen et al. 1985, Wimmer & Perner, 1983)

Compared to the previous visual perspective-taking activity, the cognitive perspective-taking activity is a little more difficult – and also more interesting. Moving beyond the five senses, the students discover how they "automatically" keep track of what another person knows - based on their knowledge of that person's experiences. This can be a very intriguing activity for elementary students, as they discover that people make very accurate guesses about what others know and/or are thinking. This ability helps people to predict the actions and responses of others. In the literature it is referred to as "theory of mind" (Baron-Cohen et al. 1985). The following activity is based on the work of Baron-Cohen (1985) and Wimmer & Perner (1983). The use of an attractive small object, and a step-by-step approach, simplify the concept:

- Ensure that all students are watching as you hide the small object (teddy bear), announcing its location in the process. *Watch closely as I hide the teddy bear in my desk drawer.*
- Ask for a volunteer (Adam).
- Direct Adam to leave the room and to remain out of view of the classroom.
- Once Adam is out of the room, silently establish everyone's attention.
- Moving slowly, remove the small item (teddy bear) from its current location (desk drawer) and place it in a new hiding place.
- Invite Adam to return to his seat, thanking him for his cooperation.

If I ask Adam to look for the teddy bear, where is he likely to look first? Why? We keep track of what other people know. Can we "read someone's mind" or do we make a guess? Actually, we make very good guesses about what other people know. Did someone teach us to do that, or is it automatic, like our senses? Add to what is already in the center of the chalkboard:

We know what other people can see, hear, taste, touch, and smell.

We make good guesses about what other people know

Affective perspective-taking activity

Accurately assessing the affective, or emotional, perspective of another person is complex, and admittedly in some situations may elude even the most sensitive adults! Here, the discussion of emotions and their related cues is kept brief and basic. This keeps the content within the developmental reach of the audience, and introduces the concept without "losing sight" of the goal of the lesson.

- Display the large photos/drawings of basic feelings.
- Identify the emotion depicted in each.
- Discuss basic cues to feelings.

Can you tell what someone is feeling? What are some clues you use to learn how someone is feeling?
Record ideas and illustrate on board:

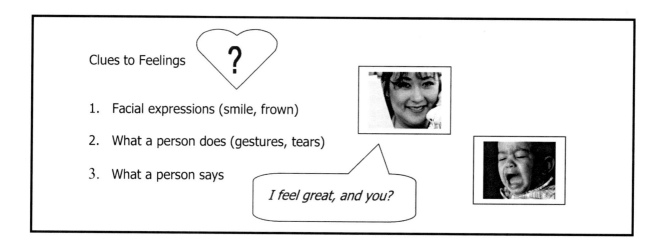

Clues to Feelings **?**

1. Facial expressions (smile, frown)
2. What a person does (gestures, tears)
3. What a person says

I feel great, and you?

We can make good guesses about how someone is feeling. We use clues to help us guess. As you have listed here, we may look to someone's face for a clue to their feelings. If someone is smiling, a good guess is that they are feeling happy. Or, if someone is frowning, we guess that they are probably feeling worried or sad. We also may look at what someone is doing. For example, when someone is crying, that gives us a big clue as to their feelings. Or, if someone is cheering and jumping up and down, it's a big clue that they are very excited. Sometimes, the clues are not as obvious. We may notice that someone who usually walks quickly is moving very slowly. Another clue to what a person is feeling is to listen to what that person says. We use these clues to make very good guesses about the feelings of others.

Look at our list in the center of the board: We know what other people see, hear, taste, touch, and smell. We guess what other people know. We guess how other people feel. This gives us lots of information about one another and helps us to work and play together. This is our sixth, or social, sense. Let's title our list, The Sixth Sense.

Add to the main list in the center of the board, including simple illustrations. Review and title the list as illustrated below:

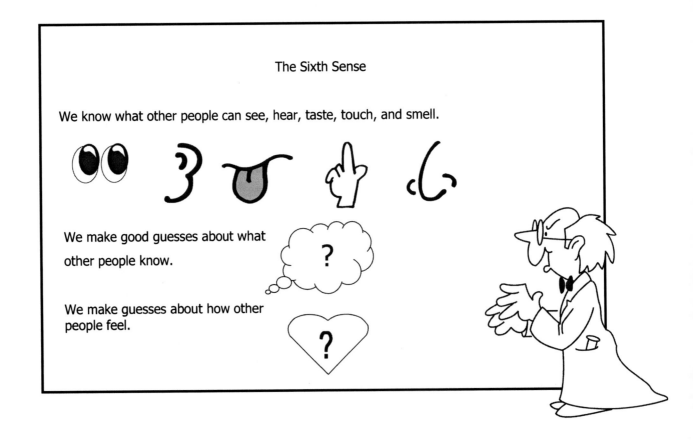

What is it like to have a Sixth Sense impairment?

In this segment of *The Sixth Sense II*, students are guided as they consider what it would be like to have a social-communication impairment. Having discussed their ability to take the perspective of other people, this ability is now put to an active test. Identifying the specific challenges of a person who cannot see or hear is likely to be easier than imagining the daily struggles of a classmate with ASD. Unlike the sense of sight or hearing, the Sixth Sense is a new concept. For this reason, students may need some guiding questions to formulate these new ideas.

What do you think it would be like to have difficulty with the Sixth Sense? I'd like to hear your ideas – let's create a list of challenges that children with Sixth Sense impairments face.

- *Would it be easy or difficult to take turns if you didn't know what others are thinking, or how they feel?*
- *Would it be easy or difficult to talk to others about something they did? Why?*
- *Would it be easy or difficult to understand why we need rules for games? Why?*
- *Would it be easy or difficult to understand why people do things? Why?*
- *Would some things that people do take you by surprise? Why?*
- *Would people frighten you sometimes?*
- *Would it be easy or difficult to make friends?*

Create a new list on the board recording the students' ideas, as illustrated below:

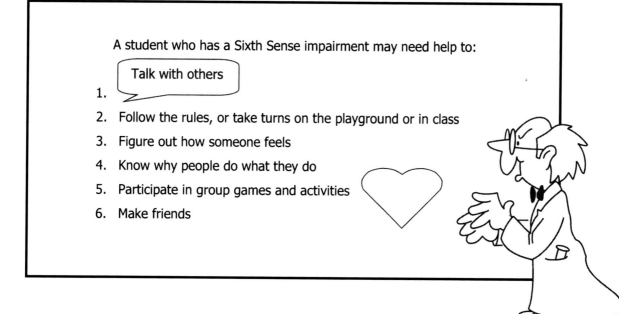

A student who has a Sixth Sense impairment may need help to:

1. Talk with others
2. Follow the rules, or take turns on the playground or in class
3. Figure out how someone feels
4. Know why people do what they do
5. Participate in group games and activities
6. Make friends

We can all use help with these skills sometimes. In our class, Andrew may need help more often. Andrew has difficulty with the Sixth Sense. Andrew also has many wonderful talents and skills. For example, you probably have seen how well Andrew reads. You may have seen his skill on the computer! Andrew may be able to help some of us with reading or the computer. In the same way, we can help Andrew with the Sixth Sense. That's what being a member of this class is all about – it's important to help one another. Next, we'll talk about how we can help Andrew.

How can we help?

Creating a list of ideas to assist a classmate with ASD is the final segment of *The Sixth Sense II*. This is a real opportunity to "pull everything together"; it is the "grand finale" of the entire lesson. It is also an opportunity to add important personal detail - for students to share behaviors they have observed and consider them in light of what they have learned. Stressing confidentiality reinforces the responsibility inherent in sharing personal information with others. This activity gives practical application to the general information and specific concerns, and supports students as they take ownership of an important part of the social solution. Ultimately, the process followed in this final step - pulling social information together to arrive at new solutions – is a prototype for learning and applying social understanding with other people in a variety of settings.

It is no surprise that many of the lists created earlier in the lesson can support students as they develop their list of helpful responses. First, it may be helpful to open this activity by praising the students' previous success in creating a list of ideas to help someone who is blind or deaf (p. 2), and provides a model for the current task. Second, inviting students to review their description of the Sixth Sense (p. 7) assists them as they make the connection between "what it would be like" and "helpful ideas." Finally, the list of challenges developed in the previous activity provides a frame of reference for identifying new ideas to assist their classmate:

Earlier you listed what it might be like if you could not see (hear). You had some wonderful ideas about how you can assist someone who cannot see (hear). Let's look at the list you developed. One idea is to help that student get around on the playground. Another is to keep things in place in the classroom so that classroom items will be easier to find. These are great ideas.

Understanding why Andrew sometimes has difficulty working and playing with others can make it easier for us to help him. For example, let's look at our description of the Sixth Sense. Perhaps one reason

Andrew rarely talks with others is because he doesn't know where to start – he may not be able to make those important guesses about what other people know or feel – as quickly or easily as you and I do. Keeping this in mind will help us figure out how we can help.

Let's look at the list you just developed. Here, you identified some challenges for people who have difficulty with the Sixth Sense. Using this list as a guide, try to brainstorm ideas that we can use to help Andrew in school and on the playground. For example, you said that, "A student who has a Sixth Sense impairment may need help to talk with others". I think this may be true for Andrew.

- *Have you noticed any times when Andrew has had difficulty talking with others? What happened?*
- *What are your ideas?*
- *What can we do to help Andrew?*

Guide a discussion of ideas to support Andrew and record as illustrated:

Helpful Ideas

1. Start the conversation. Ask Andrew to join us at lunch.
2. Write down the rules to games. Stay calm as Andrew learns to take turns.
3. Understand Andrew has feelings too, be friendly.
4. Help Andrew "find his place" and follow directions.
5. Be patient if Andrew picks up and runs with the base after Ben said, "Steal the base."
6. At first, ask an adult to help when playing with Andrew.

Summary

The Sixth Sense II is a lesson plan that shares accurate information about ASD with general education students. This lesson uses interesting activities and discussion to replace the "student theories" surrounding puzzling behaviors with accurate information based on autism research. This information is used to develop a list of helpful responses and student-generated solutions.

References
Baron-Cohen, S., A.M. Leslie, U.Frith (1985) Does the autistic child have a "theory of mind"? *Cognition 21,* 37-44.
Dawson, G., & Fernald, M. (1987). Perspective-taking ability and its relationship to the social behavior of autistic children. *Journal of Autism and Developmental Disorders, 17,* 487-498.
Gray, C. (1993). Taming the recess jungle. Future Horizons: Arlington.
Rubin, K. (2002). The friendship factor: Helping our children navigate their social world – and why it matters for their success and happiness. New York, NY: Viking Press.
Wimmer, H. & Perner, J. (1983). Beliefs about beliefs: representation and the constraining function of wrong beliefs in young children's understanding of deception. *Cognition, 13,* 103-28.

APPENDIX A   The Sixth Sense II: Answers to Frequently Asked Questions

What goes into a decision to use The Sixth Sense II? What factors should be considered?

It's an important process that determines if The Sixth Sense II is right for a student, his/her parents, and classroom. Pre-requisite to the success of the program is the comfort of everyone involved. Parents and professionals carefully review the lesson plan to decide if it will be beneficial, with the understanding that modifications can be made to tailor The Sixth Sense II to an individual student and situation.

In general, a decision to use The Sixth Sense II is made with consideration of the following factors:
1) Does the child know his/her diagnosis? Experience suggests that it is best a student know his/her diagnosis prior to implementing The Sixth Sense II. For more resources and information on sharing the diagnosis, see the answer to the following question, and Appendix B: Related Resources.
2) Is it possible to include the student in planning? If so, how? In most cases, it's important for the student to understand the purpose and content of the activity. Often, soon after a student learns of his/her diagnosis, The Sixth Sense is implemented in his/her classroom.
3) Have other students in the class observed behaviors demonstrated by the student with ASD that may be confusing? Do they seem wary of behaviors that are not typical, but otherwise harmless? Providing students with information about why some behaviors occur can positively impact attitudes and acceptance, which serve as an anecdote to negative teasing.
4) Are the parents and professionals comfortable with sharing information about their student with a classroom of children? This is very important, as the attitude of the adults toward the activity will be "picked up" by students. This is an excellent time to teach the meaning of confidentiality, and to set the expectation that it will be followed, with the understanding that children may make mistakes and need to be reminded of its importance.
5) The goal is to share accurate social information. Is The Sixth Sense II the best method for this student and situation? A decision may be made to talk with students about a child's diagnosis and/or strengths and challenges, but to use an approach other than The Sixth Sense II. Parents and professionals may creatively use commercially available resources listed in Appendix B: Related Resources to reach this goal. Or, these same resources may be used with The Sixth Sense II to complement key concepts.

Ultimately, the decision to use The Sixth Sense II is made by the student and his/her parents.

Any suggestions regarding sharing the diagnosis with my child?

The decision to share information with a child about his/her diagnosis - and how to best approach it - is dependent upon a few factors. First, there is no "right age" or date on a calendar that indicates a perfect moment in time for explaining an autism continuum diagnosis to a child. A child's age, ability, social awareness, and personality may all play a role in determining *when* to explore this topic. Collectively, these factors impact on a child's *readiness* to learn more about his/her individual strengths and weaknesses. If a child is making comparisons of himself in contrast to his peers - specifically if those comparisons are related to social concerns - it may be a good time to explain the diagnosis.   One indicator that a child wants to learn more about him/herself is when the child begins asking for that type of information. If the child is ready to ask the question, she/he is ready for the answer to *that* question.

The process of sharing this information in other words *how* to explain the diagnosis in general, mirrors the experience of all children as they discover their individual talents and challenges. For example, Peter shares the frustration of not being able to solve math problems as accurately or quickly as the child who sits next to him. Peter is reassured that while he may need to work a little harder at math to achieve the same end, others may need to practice for hours to run as fast as Peter – and may never catch up! In the same way a typical child learns about personal talents and challenges, so, too, can the child with ASD learn it is okay to learn social concepts at his/her own pace. Discovering the strengths and weaknesses that comprise the unique human package that is *you* is a part of growing up. So while the initial thought of sharing a diagnosis may be a little intimidating for parents, looking to what we know about typical children often provides a few guideposts.

The challenge for parents and professionals is to answer a child's questions as they emerge… *and nothing more*. This task is not as simple as it may appear at face value, as it requires 1) careful consideration of the child's question and 2) a quick sifting through lots of information to identify what the child wants and needs to know now. This leads to a reassuring realization: explaining an autism spectrum diagnosis occurs as a *process* that spans years. This answer will grow along with the complexity of a child's questions, gaining detail and depth over time. No need to paint the whole picture, instead, this first step is simply to introduce the paint box.

Articles and resources are available to guide the efforts of parents and professionals as they introduce and explore a diagnosis on the autism spectrum with a child. For example, *Pictures of Me* (Gray, 1996) is a Social Story that introduces a child to his/her personality, talents, and diagnosis via a series of activities completed by the child, his parents, and professionals (optional). Pictures of Me first appeared in *The Morning News* in the fall of 1996. Included in the same issue are other articles, including one by parents, Ellen Tanis and Debi Donaldson, and others by Dr. Tony Attwood and Edna Smith, Ph.D., related to helping a child, friends and family understand the diagnosis. (For a full reference and ordering information for the fall 1996 issue of The Morning News, see Appendix B, p. 17). In the Spring-Summer 2002 issue of The Morning News (originally surrounding this rip-out section), a parent, Laurel Hoekman, describes the experience of sharing the diagnosis with her two sons, Benjamin and Nathan (pp. 2-6).

If Pictures of Me is the paint box, other resources help parents and professionals sketch in details and add color to a child's understanding of his/her diagnostic picture over time. The workbook, *Aspergers… What Does It Mean to Me* (Faherty, 2000) has the potential of a great friend in the self-discovery process. It provides systematic exploration of several topics, one step at a time, patiently guiding a child and his/her team in their efforts to understand the diagnosis. (See Appendix B for reference and ordering information).

Once a decision to use The Sixth Sense is made, what's the next step?

The most important "next step" is to use the lesson plan as a *guide:* review it and if necessary revise the plan to meet the needs of everyone involved. Consider making general revisions to the content and activities, and pay attention to the suggested script and wording of key concepts. For example, Dr. Tony Attwood suggests that it is not necessary to mention the specific diagnosis in the course of The Sixth Sense. Instead, he suggests placing the emphasis on developing sensitivity to the experience of the student with ASD. Another possible revision is to avoid any reference to a specific student, instead focusing on assisting *any student* who has difficulty playing and working with others. The drawback to this is "watering down" the focus to such an extent that the original intent dissolves, in which case the opportunity to create a supportive learning environment for the student with ASD is missed.

In addition to taking care to tailor the lesson plan, it's important not to overlook practical considerations. The Sixth Sense II can help a team determine *what* information to include and *how* to present it, but what about *when* and *where?* School and classroom schedules can be complicated. Select a time slot that is not in competition with an activity or subject that is highly popular with the students. This helps to ensure that students will be focused on the task at hand, undistracted by "where they would rather be" at the time. Also, try to select a time when most children will be present, including classroom leaders. This can be a challenge since many children often are absent from a classroom to attend a variety of other programs, from special education to accelerated classes to supportive services. Since the topic is one impacting the classroom community, attendance is important.

Do you have any suggestions to individualize The Sixth Sense II to a student and his/her classmates?

Imagining The Sixth Sense II as a finished garment, there are several "seams" along which alterations can be made to tailor the information to meet the needs of 1) the student with ASD, and 2) his/her classmates.

Needs of the student with ASD   The expression of autism is unique in each student with the diagnosis. This dictates revisions in the information included in the lesson. First, understanding that social skills are not impaired in a "blanket fashion" in ASD, it's important for parents and professionals to consider the student's individual social profile when determining what to include. The child's social strengths can be mentioned along with the challenges. For example, Mr. Andrews' fourth graders are learning about their academically-talented classmate, Austin, and his social-communication challenges. In the course of the perceptual perspective-taking activity described on page 3, Mr. Andrews mentions that, like his classmates, Austin also has the ability to readily identify what others can see, or hear. Later, in the course of the affective perspective-taking task, Mr. Andrews indicates that *this* is where Austin often has the most difficulty.

Challenges in sensory processing are frequently a factor in autism, and sharing this information with classmates may be important to understanding some behaviors. *When* to share information about sensory challenges with classmates may not be as obvious at it first seems. For example, Mr. Andrews decides it's important to explain Austin's hyper-sensitivity to sound. Initially, it seems logical to mention this during the perceptual perspective-taking task (p. 3). Later Mr. Andrews changes his mind, electing to keep the focus on typical perspective-taking abilities at this early point in the lesson. Instead, Mr. Andrews elects to mention Austin's auditory sensitivity later in the lesson, after the focus turns from typical social cognition to Austin's challenges. Thus, Austin's hyper-sensitivity to school alarms and bells is mentioned as the students discuss how they can help Austin.

Needs of the classmates   Custom fitting The Sixth Sense II to the student with ASD is the first step. Tailoring the lesson to the needs of the audience is the second. While The Sixth Sense II is applicable for students in second through sixth grade, there's a "social world of developmental difference" between the ages of seven and twelve, or eight and ten for that matter. Knowing the audience affirms their own daily social experiences and thus, captivates their interest.

A teacher knows the social developmental profile of his/her audience; The Sixth Sense II is the perfect opportunity to put that information to practical use. For example, if presenting The Sixth Sense II to an early elementary audience, a teacher will emphasize concepts and provide examples directly related to the experience of seven and eight year olds. At this age, a "friend" is someone who helps you, plays with you, is nice to you - observable acts and basic character traits are the defining factors. Therefore, the teacher can draw his/her examples of friendship from that second grade classroom: describing offers of assistance and acts of kindness. In contrast, it would be potentially confusing to encourage seven-year olds to "always be there" for one another, when their play interactions and relationships are often fleeting and undecided. Presenting social information that children recognize increases interest, affirms their own experience, and helps to set reasonable expectations for behavior.

My experience with The Sixth Sense over the years has resulted in many positive outcomes, along with a few results that were not expected. Sometimes, despite our careful planning to avoid pitfalls, efforts to individualize the plan to the needs of the student with ASD, and consideration of the developmental level of the audience, we're taken by surprise. After all, that's to be expected working with children. One unexpected outcome has occurred so frequently over the last nine years that I have decided it deserves mention.

At the completion of The Sixth Sense students are often dismissed to the playground or their next class. This is followed by a predictable scramble of chairs sliding back, desks opening and closing, books dropping, all which is accompanied by student conversation. The social dust clears and there - quietly standing motionless long past the student scatter - is one student pointing toward the board and saying, "Mrs. Gray, you described me, too."

In one instance in my nine years of experience with this lesson plan, that turned out to be the case. A child came forward at the close of The Sixth Sense II and was later formally diagnosed. More often, a formal diagnosis is not the outcome. What I believe happens is this: the social challenge I describe is recognized by children who for one reason or another - but certainly not due to the autism spectrum - are lonely, and struggle to establish friendships. As The Sixth Sense for most students increases understanding of peers with ASD, for a few the lesson holds up a most unexpected mirror.

Children who recognize themselves in the course of this lesson deserve our attention and concern. It's important to ensure they are put in contact with educational staff that can determine the severity of their social challenge and provide assistance and support if it is indicated. At Jenison Public Schools, that would be the child's general-education teacher, school counselor, principal, parents, and/or the resources in special education. The point is to be aware that some students may recognize aspects of their own experience in the description of the social sense.

Should the child with the ASD be present when The Sixth Sense is implemented in his class?

In my experience, I have seen the lesson plan completed successfully both ways – with the student present, and with the student engaged in an activity in another location. The answer to this question is influenced by many factors, including the age of the student, the personality of the student (and the class), the student's level of social awareness, and the desires of the parents. These factors should be discussed among parents, professionals, and in many cases the student, prior to implementation. The decision ultimately rests with the parents and their student.

In your opinion, who best implements The Sixth Sense?

Over the last seven years, I have been aware of many adults leading The Sixth Sense, representing roles from parent to psychologist to teacher. As a result, I have developed a theory: The person best suited to implement The Sixth Sense, especially when the long-term impact is considered, is the *general-education* teacher. By leading the activity, the general education teacher demonstrates that he/she understands and values the information. In contrast, a "guest speaker" conducting The Sixth Sense may be unknown to the students, and more importantly, disappear at its conclusion. In this case, the information originates from – and returns to – a location other than the classroom. In addition, a guest speaker has little knowledge of the "classroom personality", or the individual factors of each of its members. For this reason, The Sixth Sense II is designed to be easy to understand and implement, with additional information that general education professionals need.

Sometimes, the general education teacher feels more comfortable if another person with expertise in autistic spectrum disorders implements The Sixth Sense. This can still be effective, with a few words of caution. If a "guest speaker" is used, it's important for the teacher to be a present and active participant throughout the lesson, and a leader in a short discussion regarding what has been learned, and what it means to the class as a whole. Sometimes, the school principal also attends and learns along with the students. His/her presence can 1) underscore the importance of the activity and 2) reinforce the expectation that students will apply the information in all school-related contexts.

The Sixth Sense II is appropriate for use with students ages 7-12. There is still a need for similar programs for early childhood and secondary students. Do you have any suggestions related to sharing these concepts with other students? Is there a Sixth Sense Junior or Senior?

Currently, a trip to the book store can make The Sixth Sense II concepts available to other audiences. For very young audiences, there are wonderful newly released children's books that foster self-esteem, mutual respect, and positive conflict resolution with younger audiences. A careful search for children's books that share accurate social information is likely to be more productive now than compared to even a few short years ago. Some of these books also have accompanying brief, inexpensive parent/teacher guides that outline supplemental activities. In this way, each book introduces an important social concept(s) that is readily applied to the child's own experience. Many of these resources are available from Free Spirit Publishing. For more information, see Appendix B: Related Resources/Young Children.

I recently discovered *Knowing Me, Knowing You* (Espeland, 2001) a new resource for students ages 12-18 to increase awareness of individual personalities and strategies for working effectively with others. Many of the concepts in this book are "advanced shadows" of The Sixth Sense II. The book is creatively developed with an instrument for students to use to determine their "preferred social response style". For a full reference and more information see Appendix B: Related Resources/Secondary Students.

After The Sixth Sense activity is completed, is that it? Or, are there other activities/strategies that reinforce these concepts throughout the year?

Many of the concepts in The Sixth Sense are important to a positive and supportive classroom community for *all* students, not just the included classmate. Just as Social Stories are "right at home" alongside a variety of instructional strategies used to educate children with ASD, so too will The Sixth Sense complement all of the efforts of parents and professionals to build socially comfortable classroom environments. There is a wide variety of materials and resources available to professionals that promote a positive classroom climate. One activity/resource we've developed to assist in this area is *The Classroom Catalog*.

The Classroom Catalog could be considered a "social registry" of all of the students in a classroom. A typical child observes, listens, and gradually learns about the children in their classroom; their preferred activities, likes and dislikes, weaknesses and strengths. For a variety of reasons, a child with ASD has difficulty accessing this information - information that is so readily apparent to their classmates. This makes it difficult if not impossible to identify a good potential playmate. While independent access to information about the child in the second row, third seat, may be a challenge for a child with ASD, s/he may be able to understand and use the information if it is presented in a meaningful format. This provides the rationale for a creating a "catalog" of children as a social reference, a "Who's Who at Recess".

In addition to providing information for the child with ASD, the Classroom Catalog is likely to be helpful for *all* students. Similar to *Student of the Week* bulletin boards, students share information about

My name is _Angela Griffin_____. I am ___8___ years old.
My birthday is every year on _March 5_. This year, my birthday falls on a _Tuesday_.

This is a photograph of me.

**This is a picture I drew of myself on the playground.
I like to _play ball_ on the playground.**

I am an important member of my class. In my class, students help one another succeed. One subject
that I really enjoy is _science_____. A subject that is usually easy for me is
_math_____. A subject that I would be willing to help others with is
math or science. Others in my class may be able to help me with my difficult subjects.

I asked my parent /caregiver to tell me one word that describes my personality. It is _happy_
After school or on the weekend, one thing I really like to do is _play outside_
One book or story that I really like is _Charlotte's Web_
In my opinion, the best movie / television show is _The Lion King_.
(Choose one) I have a pet. It is a _Cat_. My pet's name is _Cinders_
        I do not have a pet. Someday, I might like to have a _____ for a pet.
When I grow up, I would like to be a _doctor or scientist_.
One thing I would like others to know about me is _that I can sew_

themselves with their classmates in a resource that is available all year. The catalog provides *all* students with information that may otherwise go undetected, *and an opening* to initiate contact with students with similar interests. For example, a new student moves in over the summer and is approached by a classmate, "I saw in the Classroom Catalog that you played soccer at your school in Texas before you moved…want to play soccer with us today?" In addition, listing academic strengths is great for self esteem, and emphasizes the role all students can play assisting others. If Jamie is terrific at writing poetry, she can list herself as someone willing to help others in that area, while using the catalog herself to choose someone who may help her raise her grade in mathematics.

The information included in the *Classroom Catalog is at the discretion of the teacher, and possibly the students. A teacher may design the page *or* use class discussion to determine what information to include. Pages may be completed in class or at home to include parents in the project. Completed pages are inserted into plastic sleeves to ensure durability and assembled into a notebook with a clear plastic cover. To bring renewed attention to the catalog and its uses throughout the year: 1) students may take turns creating a new cover for the catalog once a week; 2) teachers may use it to randomly select students for special tasks or to provide answers, placing a small sticky note tab on each page to indicate which students have been selected; or 3) visitors to the classroom may be handed the catalog to introduce the students (parent permission may be advisable).

A blank version of the sample Classmate Catalog form (above) is available on the following page. Restricted permission to copy this form is granted for non-profit group and classroom use.

My name is _____. I am _____ years old.

My birthday is every year on_____. This year, my birthday falls on a _____.

This is a photograph of me.

This is a picture I drew of myself on the playground. I like to _____ on the playground.

I am an important member of my class. In my class, students help one another succeed. One subject

that I really enjoy is _____. A subject that is usually easy for me is

_____. A subject that I would be willing to help others with is

_____. Others in my class may be able to help me with my difficult subjects.

I asked my parent /caregiver to tell me one word that describes my personality. It is _____.

After school or on the weekend, one thing I really like to do is_____.

One book or story that I really like is _____.

In my opinion, the best movie / television show is _____.

(Choose one) I have a pet. It is a _____. My pet's name is _____.

I do not have a pet. Someday, I might like to have a _____ for a pet.

When I grow up, I would like to be a _____.

One thing I would like others to know about me is _____.

APPENDIX B: Related Resources

The resources listed in this appendix are representative of books for children that teach the value of human differences, the challenge facing children with special needs, the feelings of those excluded from social alliances, and the value of acceptance and peaceful conflict resolution. These resources may be used to reinforce, expand, and review concepts that are central to The Sixth Sense II. They are listed alphabetically by the author's last name. In the descriptions of these resources italicized font indicates the title(s) of additional resources found in the book, or selected passages of text. Resources that present similar concepts for age groups outside the range of The Sixth Sense II (early childhood ages 3-6 and secondary students age 12-18) are listed in separate sections at the conclusion of this appendix.

Edwards, A. (2001) Taking Autism to School. Plainview, NY: JayJo Books. Ages 5-10. 28 pages with color illustrations. Contains an autism quiz, *Ten Tips for Teachers,* and a list of *Additional Resources.*

➢ Angel introduces her friend, Sam, to the reader. Sam has autism. Concepts covered in the book include a description of behaviors and reasons why they occur, learning style and commonly used supports (for example, a picture schedule), as well as how Sam is similar to other children. *Many doctors and other important people are learning new things about autism every day. Our class is learning more about autism too. The more we learn, the better we can understand Sam and his feelings. Understanding is what being friends is all about. I'm glad Sam is my friend. I hope Sam can be your friend too!* (p. 21)

Faherty, C. (2000) What Does It Mean To Me? Arlington, TX: Future Horizons. Suggest middle childhood to adolescence. 300 pages with black and white illustrations. Includes a preface for parents and professionals.

➢ A step-by-step, easy to follow and reader friendly road to self discovery for youth with autistic spectrum disorders. Using an interactive workbook format with opportunities for sentence completion by the reader, this resource is an invaluable tool that results in a comprehensive book about "me". Topics include but are not limited to: sensory issues, communication, home, school, people, friends, and feelings. Parents and professionals will discover that they also learn much that they did not know about their student!

Gainer, C. (1998) I'm Like You, You're Like Me: A Child's Book About Understanding and Celebrating Each Other! Minneapolis, MN: Free Spirit Publishing. Ages 3-8. 41 pages with color illustrations. Leader's Guide also available. One book from a series with related topics.

➢ A book for young children about human variation. Beginning with physical similarities and differences, the text and illustrations gradually proceed to more advanced/abstract topics, like feelings. *I feel accepted when you invite me to your home to play. Or when you want to be my buddy as we line up for playground time. I feel accepted when you say I'm your friend.* (p. 20).

Galvin, M. (2001) Otto Learns About His Medicine: A Story About Medication for Children with ADHD. Washington, D.C: Magination Press / American Psychological Association. Ages 4-8. 32 pages with color illustrations. Contains a concluding *Note to Parents for the Third Edition.*

➢ Using cars as an analogy, the author describes the difficulty that Otto, a young car, has paying attention at home and school. Otto's parents, teacher, and physician work together as a "pit crew" to help Otto. He learns new strategies to keep organized, and receives medication from the doctor. *He also asked if he could look under Otto's hood. He checked the oil. He checked the headlights. He checked everything. Dr. Beemer said, "Otto, I think Dr. Wheeler is right. There is a medicine that may help you." This medicine would help Otto keep still long enough to pay attention long enough to learn what he needed to know* (p. 20).

Gehret, J. (1996) The Don't-give-up Kid and Learning Differences. Fairport, N.Y: Verbal Images Press. 34 pages with black and white illustrations. Contains a *Parent Resource Guide* and a *Bibliography For Talking to Kids About LD.*

➢ This is the story about Alex, a child with a learning disability. Alex feels defeated in his struggle to learn to read, until he is introduced to Mrs. Baxter who provides an environment and strategies that help Alex learn to read: *"Then she told me a story about Thomas Edison, the inventor. One of his inventions took 10,000 tries before it would work. One day he was asked, "How does it feel to have failed 10,000 times?" "I didn't fail 10,000 times," Mr. Edison answered. "I succeeded at finding 10,000 ways that didn't work." After many more tries, his invention was a big success. If I want to be like Mr. Edison, I have to keep trying too.* (pp 14-15).

Gray, C. (1996) Pictures of Me. Jenison, MI: Jenison Public Schools. Contact: Karen Lind, Jenison High School, 2140 Bauer Road, Jenison, MI. 49428. (616) 457-8955. Email: gcenter@gateway.net

➢ *Pictures of Me* is a Social Story that guides the process of sharing a diagnosis on the autism spectrum with a child. Parents, selected professionals, and the child complete a series of lists that introduce the child to his/her personality, talents, and diagnosis. In addition, everyone draws a picture of the child that emphasizes his/her strengths and positive assets. The Story closes with a description of the people who can help as the child continues to grow and gather information.

Lalli, J. (1997) I Like Being Me: Poems for Children About Feeling Special, Appreciating Others, and Getting Along. Minneapolis: MN: Free Spirit Publishing. 53 pages with black and white photographs. Suggested ages preschool through early elementary.

➢ What a fun book for children! Topics addressed via short, simple poems include: making choices, feelings, self-esteem, honesty, cooperation, sharing, manners, repairing a social error, and appreciating the perspectives of others. Though some of the concepts may be too difficult for very young children, the short, entertaining text and many developmentally appropriate topics make it a great resource for a wide audience. A sample poem titled, *Someone Else's Chair* reads: *Want to learn about each other? Want to show how much you care? Just imagine what's it's like, To sit in someone else's chair* (p. 28).

Mitchell, L. (1999) Different Just Like Me. Watertown, MA: Charlesbridge Publishing. 28 pages. Color illustrations. Suggest preschool and early elementary grades. Awards: *Kid's Pick of the Lists* (ABA), Spring, 1999; *Early Childhood News Director's Choice Award,* 2000; *Notable Social Studies Trade Books for Young People,* 2000.

➢ In one week April will be visiting her grandmother. On each day of the week prior to the visit, April encounters someone who is different, just like her. On these pages, only the people in the illustrations are depicted in full color, the rest is black and white. This draws attention to the characters and their physical or personal differences, while the text notes the similarities between April and the characters. For example, an illustration of a woman in a wheelchair handing a paper towel to April, is accompanied by this text: *Before we left, I went to the rest room. While I was standing at the sink, a lady came out of the biggest stall and washed her hands. I smiled, and she said hello. She handed me a paper towel and then dried her hands, just like me.* (p. 13)

Murkoff, H. (2001) What to Expect at a Play Date. U.S.A: Harper Collins Publishers. 22 pages with color illustrations. Suggest preschool through early elementary. Includes *A Word to Parents* guide.

➢ This book uses a question and answer format to share basic step-by-step information about a play date. The information and format is likely to be very helpful to children with autistic spectrum disorders. Topics include: *What's a play date? Who will be at the play date? Who will I see at the play date? What will I do at the play date? Why do I have to share my toys? What if my friend doesn't share? What if my friend and I do not want to do the same thing? and When will the play date be over?* (selected titles quoted from text).

Polland, B. K. (2000) We Can Work it Out: Conflict Resolution for Children. Berkeley, CA: Tricycle Press. 63 pages with color photographs. Suggest elementary. Includes a preface for parents and professionals.

> ➢ This book can serve as a guide to discussions with children about conflicts and their effective resolution. Topics include: kindness, compliments, criticism, taking responsibility, exclusion and inclusion, honesty, friendship, jealousy, and acceptance. The social concepts that are introduced would be applicable throughout the elementary grades, despite the initial impression that the book may give as an early elementary resource.

Roca, N. & Curto, R.M. (2001) Friendship, from your old friends to your new friends. English version published by Barron's Educational Series, Inc: New York. Original title in Catalan: L'Amistat, dels amics d'abans als amics d'ara, published by Gemser Publications: Barcelona, Spain (2000). 35 pages. Color illustrations. Includes *Activities,* a section that describes several games to play with friends, and *Guidelines for Parents.*

> ➢ This is the story of John, who has recently moved and finds himself "between friends". The book emphasizes the value of former friendships, and the feelings of loss associated with moving. John spends some time playing alone, eventually venturing out to make new social connections. Along the way, the text identifies several social issues in childhood: personality differences among friends; "best" friends; peer conflict; apologies; exclusion; loneliness; maintaining old friendships; the steps to form new social contacts, and jealousy. John makes a new friend, Mark, who has several other friends: *Mark has a lot of friends in this neighborhood, so he always has someone to play with. Sometimes John is a little jealous because he wishes he didn't have to share his friend with anybody else..."* (p. 22). Considering most children will recognize John's temporary social predicament, this book could lay the groundwork for The Sixth Sense II, and the discussion of a peer whose social isolation may be more severe or long lasting.

Rubin, K. H. (2002) The Friendship Factor. New York, NY: Viking Press. A resource for parents and professionals. 322 pages.

> ➢ This book is a research-based guide to the development of social relationships in childhood and adolescence and the multi-faceted role they play in a child's development, with practical advice for parents and professionals. From the inside front cover: *Dr. Kenneth Rubin has discovered that our children's abilities to navigate their social worlds shape all aspects of their emotional and intellectual growth. ...Dr. Rubin has also discovered that the ability to connect socially is something children learn and can develop over time.* For parents and professionals working on behalf of children with autism spectrum disorders (ASD), Dr. Rubin's work is a valuable resource that accurately describes the social landscape of childhood and its interaction with a child's personality and inherited disposition. Perhaps more importantly, Rubin's book will remind those working on behalf of children with ASD that a child with ASD is *first* a child with a unique personality. To those who reflect thoughtfully between the lines, Rubin's book raises interesting new questions for those of us working on behalf of children with ASD, potentially opening new doors for the development of social curricula.

Sheindlin, J. (2001) You Can't Judge a Book by Its Cover: Cool Rules for School. USA: Cliff Street Books / Harper Collins Publishers. Ages 7-12. 94 pages with black and white illustrations.

> ➢ Judge Judy Sheindlin opens this book with a note <u>To the Kids</u>: *Adults seem to have little sayings for everything. But what do they really mean? They sound very interesting, but how do you use them in your everyday life to solve problems and make the right choices* (p. 1). Using a format that presents children with problem situations with four possible answers, Judge Judy explains the meaning of several phrases. Children learn important life lessons at the same time, among them concepts directly related to The Sixth Sense II.

Twachtman-Cullen, D. (1998) Trevor Trevor. Cromwell, CT: Starfish Press. Suggest early elementary grades. 41 pages and a preface, with color illustrations and "paper doll" Trevor.

> This is the story of Trevor, a boy with autism included in a second grade classroom. Many of the students do not understand some of Trevor's behaviors, as demonstrated by some of their responses to him. In a puzzle competition with another school, Trevor's talents cause his classmates to view him in a new light. *Mrs. Grayley looked at the faces of her students, and for the very first time, she saw admiration for the little boy they had teased so often. She now knew that her Puzzlemania idea had been a good one, after all* (p. 37).

Walker, A. (1991) Finding the Green Stone. New York, NY: Harcourt, Brace, & Co. Suggest early to middle elementary grades. 34 pages with color paintings by Catherine Deeter.

> This children's book with beautiful illustrations can serve as the impetus for activities stressing the importance of a positive classroom community. In a town where everyone has a glowing green stone, Johnny's mean spirited behavior causes him to lose his green stone. His family and friends help Johnny search for his missing green stone, until Johnny discovers he must find it on his own in his heart. A teacher can translate the concepts into practical application within the classroom, for example, dropping a green stone (marble) in a glass jar whenever acts of kindness or assistance are observed.

Early Childhood

Recognizing that The Sixth Sense II is too advanced and lengthy for very young audiences, the following resources may be used to teach similar concepts to children ages 3-7. The books in this list cover topics ranging from how people are similar and unique, self awareness and self esteem, basic feelings, acceptance, making choices, and repairing social mistakes. Many of the books contain notes to parents and professionals, and a few have separate teacher's guides that list a variety of related activities. Collectively, these books represent the growing number of wonderful resources available to build the earliest – and most basic - social studies units. (The reader is also encouraged to review the books listed on pages 17-19 for other possible titles.)

Gainer, C. (1998) I'm Like You, You're Like Me: A Child's Book About Understanding and Celebrating Each Other! Minneapolis, MN: Free Spirit Publishing. Ages 3-8. 41 pages with color illustrations. Leader's Guide also available. One book from a series with related topics.

> A book for young children about human variation. Beginning with physical similarities and differences, the text and illustrations gradually proceed to more advanced/abstract topics, like feelings. *I feel accepted when you invite me to your home to play. Or when you want to be my buddy as we line up for playground time. I feel accepted when you say I'm your friend.* (p. 20).

Grobel Intrater, R. (2000) Two Eyes, A Nose, and a Mouth. New York, NY: Scholastic, Inc. Suggest early childhood. 26 pages with large full color photographs of many varied faces.

> A very basic look at the variety of faces in the world, with wonderful close up photographs of the differences and similarities described in the text. The author uses a rhymical and rhyming format, with a few sentences a page. A nice introduction to how each person is unique, and how that makes the world very interesting. *Some eyes are shaped liked almonds. Others are big and round. And what about the eyebrows? Why all kinds can be found* (pp 5-8).

Hofbauer, M. P. (2000) Couldn't We Make a Difference? Hong Kong: Greene Bark Press. Ages 3-8. 28 pages with color illustrations.

> A story about social acceptance with simple, engaging rhyming text and clear illustrations. The book positively presents a variety of topics, including: taking another's perspective, human

differences, conflict resolution, cooperation, and helping others. *Then, couldn't we help each other, to walk or climb or stand? I could give you a leg up, You could give me a hand.* (p. 19).

Payne, L. M. (1997) We Can Get Along: A Child's Book of Choices. Minneapolis, MN: Free Spirit Publishing. Preschool-early elementary. 30 pages with color illustrations. Leader's Guide also available.

➢ A basic book about making social choices and conflict resolution. The book opens with descriptions of negative interactions and the resulting feelings, proceeding to suggestions or more positive responses. The description of friendship may be more developmentally suited for students who are much older. The text may be confusing for students with autistic spectrum disorders.

Payne, L. M. (1994) Just Because I Am: A Child's Book of Affirmation. Minneapolis, MN: Free Spirit Publishing. Preschool-early elementary. 26 pages with color illustrations. Leader's Guide also available.

➢ This book is a very basic introduction to several self awareness and social concepts, including: body awareness, feelings, safety, self-esteem, making social mistakes, and making decisions. *I am myself. I am special and unique. My body is a part of me. My feelings are a part of me. My thoughts are a part of me. My needs are a part of me. All of these things make up a special person... Me* (p. 25-26).

Rogers, F. (2000) Let's Talk About It: Extraordinary Friends. New York, N.Y: Penguin Putnam Books for Young Readers. Estimated ages 3-7. 30 pages with color photographs.

➢ This book covers several concepts related to social understanding and peer acceptance with an accurate, straight forward and practical approach. It is creatively organized. For example, the children who served as models for the photographs are introduced on the first page. *Sometimes it can be hard to remember how much people are alike, especially when you meet someone who doesn't walk or talk or learn the same way you do. You might be curious. Sometimes you might have questions... and other times you might not* (pp. 6-7).

Secondary Students

Espeland, P. (2001) Knowing Me, Knowing You: The I-Sight Way to Understand Yourself and Others. Minneapolis, MN: Free Spirit Publishing and Inscape Publishing, Inc. Ages 12-18. 110 pages. Contains *I-Sight*, "the *Personal Profile System* (Minneapolis, MN: Inscape Publishing) developed for ages 12-18, and "customized for teens with new research that ensure its validity and reliability" (back cover). Includes permission to copy the instrument and related activities for group use.

➢ This book is creatively organized to guide teens through the rationale and application of the *I-Sight instrument*. This instrument provides teens with insight into how they frequently respond to people and social situations, then identifies "things to look out for" to successfully interact with others. With modification and clarification of abstract terms, this instrument may be useful for teens with autistic spectrum disorders. Especially interesting is the emphasis on increasing awareness of how others may interpret and respond to each personality type; and the learning of "flex behaviors" to minimize conflicts and maximize social success. *Knowing Me, Knowing You* goes beyond I-Sight to offer practical suggestions for making it part of your life.

CPSIA information can be obtained at www.ICGtesting.com

233172LV00001BC/1/P